invite
PRESS

ERMA METZGER
with DAN METZGER

HOW *not* TO RUIN CHRISTMAS

DAILY DEVOTIONAL

invite PRESS
Plano, Texas

How NOT to Ruin Christmas Daily Devotional

Copyright © 2024 by Erma Metzger and Dan Metzger

All rights reserved.

No part of this work may be reproduced or transmitted in any form or by any means, electronic or mechanical, including photocopying and recording, or by any information storage or retrieval system, except as may be expressly permitted by the 1976 Copyright Act or in writing from the publisher. Requests for permission can be addressed to Permissions, Invite Press, P.O. Box 260917, Plano, TX 75026.

This book is printed on acid-free, elemental chlorine-free paper.

ISBN 978-1-96326-5-16-3

Scriptures are from THE HOLY BIBLE, NEW INTERNATIONAL VERSION®, NIV® Copyright © 1973, 1978, 1984, 2011 by Biblica, Inc.® Used by permission. All rights reserved worldwide.

24 25 26 27 28 29 30 31 32 33 —10 9 8 7 6 5 4 3 2 1

MANUFACTURED in the UNITED STATES of AMERICA

To my husband, Dean; our sons, Dan, Kyle, and Jake; and their spouses and children. You all bring more joy, love, and meaning to my life than I ever could have imagined.

Also in memory of my sweet mom, Adelyn, who shaped my faith and understanding of grace.

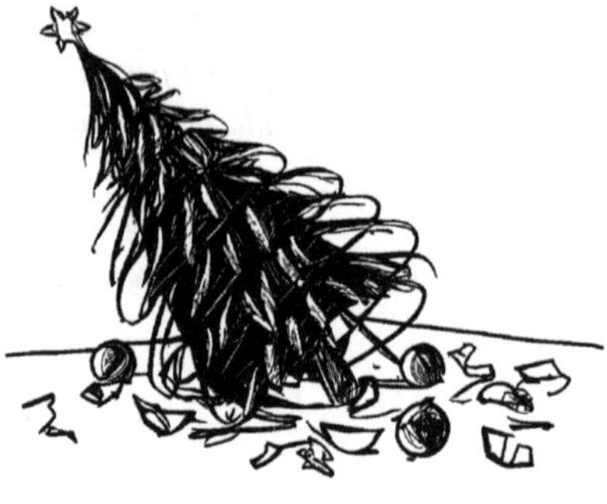

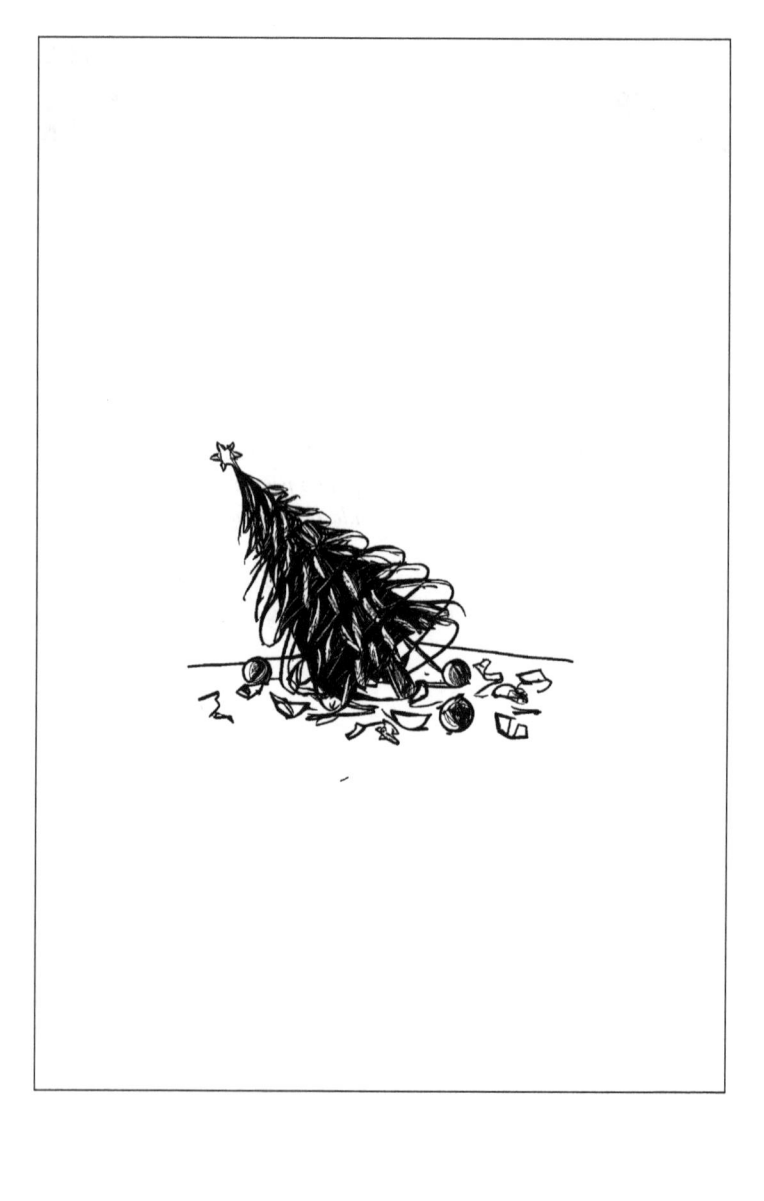

December 1

"The people walking in darkness have seen a great light. . . . For to us a child is born, to us a son is given. . . ." —Isaiah 9:2, 6

My family enjoys flipping the calendar pages throughout the year. For a number of years, our daughter-in-law, Holly, created personalized calendars for all of us with lots of pictures of our growing family. A few years ago the task of creating the calendars was passed to our middle son, Kyle, and that's when flipping the calendar pages became a form of entertainment. It still includes pictures of all of us but there is also a theme that flows throughout the year. One year he made sure there was a picture of him on every single page, including some that cropped everyone else out of the picture, leaving just him. This past year, on each family member's birthdate, instead of naming and picturing that person, he found a celebrity of some sort who shared the same birthdate and put their picture on that day instead.

But I must admit, aside from the enjoyment of the pictures and the humor that goes along with our family calendars, some months I'm not as thrilled to turn the calendar to the next month as others. Every year I am less fond of the cold and gray winter months and much happier to turn the page to June, July, and August with thoughts of sunshine, warmth, gardens, and lots of time outdoors. Positive or negative, it's really all about the anticipation of what the month might hold for me.

So we've turned the calendar to December. (By the way, Kyle replaced his own daughter's picture with Johnny Manziel's on her birthdate this month. But seriously . . .) Pause for a moment to consider this question: What are you anticipating that this month will hold for you? Long lines at the checkout, spending more than you should, obligatory gift-giving, office parties, and extended family gatherings with the white-elephant exchanges you greatly dislike? What if this year, even though that list might hold true to some extent, you could experience this Christmas season in a way that is life-giving rather than as a time that leaves you frazzled and frustrated?

We are embarking on the season of Advent. The word *advent* means the coming or arrival of something or someone that is important or worthy of note. For Christians, Advent is the time leading up to Christmas Day, when we celebrate once again the arrival of the Christ child into the world. To truly experience this season to the fullest, we must not only look back at this historical event but anticipate and plan for Jesus' continuous coming into our world and our lives. As Dan Metzger explains in *How NOT to Ruin Christmas*, we can allow worry, conflict, misery, and selfishness to rule our lives during this time, or we can embrace the gifts of divine hope, peace, joy, and love that God has granted us through the incarnation of his only Son into the world. Throughout these coming weeks, may we open our hearts and anticipate the gifts God has in store for us this Advent season.

Heavenly Father, as we celebrate the birth of Jesus, fill our hearts with hope, knowing that through him, we have the promise of eternal life and everlasting joy.

Reflect: What are the things that most often cause you to worry at Christmastime?

December 2

"Search me, God, and know my heart; test me and know my anxious thoughts." —Psalm 139:23

My mom was an avid list-maker, and I inherited the gene. Lists give me a sense of order, and checking things off the list helps me to feel I've accomplished what I've set out to get done. When I was working as a pastor I felt it was imperative to keep a running list of things I needed to get done, and chances were, if it wasn't on the list it wouldn't happen. I recently retired, and my life now has much less of a schedule and regimen. But I still make lists; it gives me a level of comfort in my day-to-day life that I'm still accomplishing some things.

Lists during this time of year seem to be endless. I have lists of gifts to buy, food to purchase, favorite baked items to have on hand for when family arrives, and dates of concerts and special events for the calendar as I prepare for Christmas and the days leading up to it.

To fully enjoy the Christmas season, and not just endure it, we need to prepare. But I'm not just talking about making lists or shopping early to beat the crowds. I'm suggesting a preparing of our hearts. It requires some time and intention—but I guarantee you, it will be worth it. The psalmist, David, asked God to search and know his heart, and you can read over and over throughout David's writings of his deep connection with God as he poured out his heart to his Lord.

In the midst of all the preparations you are making this month for gift-giving and gatherings, take the time needed to prepare your heart for the fullness of this season. Open your heart to how the Christ of Christmas might work in you and through you in new ways to bring a little more joy to your heart and hope to the world around you. Consider putting communion with God at the top of your list each day.

Lord, in this season of anticipation, may the hope born in a manger ignite a flame of faith in our lives, reminding us of your unfailing love and mercy.

Reflect: What do you do to prepare your heart for Christmas?

December 3

"'I am the Lord's servant,' Mary answered." —Luke 1:38

The story of the life of Mary, the mother of Jesus, has always been fascinating to me. Her simple, very ordinary life was completely turned upside down at a very young age. It's hard to imagine all that could have been going on in her heart and mind when the angel, Gabriel, appeared to her and gave her the news that she was going to carry the Son of God in her womb. We've read and heard the story so many times that maybe it doesn't always impact us with the awe and wonder that it should.

The message this angel brings to her is the fulfillment of centuries of prophecy of a Messiah who would come into the world and reign for all eternity. This young girl, engaged to be married to a humble carpenter in a tiny, mostly unknown village, was chosen to birth the Messiah. And we only have record of her asking one question of this angel: "How will this be since I am a virgin?" I think I would have had a million questions and likely some excuses to try to get out of the job, such as "How in the world will anyone—including Joseph and my family—ever believe this story? And what are the chances that this baby will ever be born anyway? The law says I could be stoned for being pregnant and not married!"

But, as far as we know, Mary didn't ask a million questions or attempt to change the angel's mind. When it was explained how this was going to happen, she simply replied, "I am the

Lord's servant. May it be to me as you have said." And as quickly as the angel had arrived, the angel was gone and Mary was alone with her thoughts. While I'm sure her mind was racing and a lot of thoughts were swirling around in her brain, the best explanation for her holding it together has to be a faith in God to make this all work. In the midst of this incredible and unsettling news she was faithful and willing. Though she could not yet fully comprehend it, she was carrying the Hope of the world within her.

May we be found faithful to share the Hope of the world with the corner of the world where we live.

Gracious God, as we gather with loved ones, may the Hope of Christmas bring comfort to the broken-hearted, healing to the wounded, and restoration to weary souls.

Reflect: How do you think Mary experienced both hope and worry over the message of the angel?

December 4

"Do not be anxious about anything, but in every situation, by prayer and petition, with thanksgiving, present your requests to God." —Philippians 4:6

What keeps you up at night? Of course there are some inevitable things that will wake you from sleep—thunderstorms, having to use the bathroom, letting the dog out, holding a crying child. . . . But I'm talking about the deeper things that might keep you awake. Will we have enough money to pay for the car repairs that are desperately needed? How are we going to handle our teenager's recent change in behavior and choice of friends? How am I going to make it through another day in this job that's sucking the life out of me? What if my recent medical tests reveal bad news? Worry . . . I'm guessing you can relate. And of course—things always seem more bleak and hopeless in the middle of a dark night.

If anyone in the Christmas story had reason to worry, it would have been Mary. She was so young, and this message from the angel, Gabriel, though she was a willing servant of God, must have been overwhelming. What does scripture tell us that she did right after the angel left her? The very next verses, Luke 1:39–40, tell us, "At that time Mary got ready and hurried to a town in the hill country of Judea, where she entered Zechariah's home and greeted Elizabeth."

The angel had informed Mary that her relative, Elizabeth, was also carrying a child—though it was in her old age. Earlier in Luke 1 we read the account of the angel, Gabriel, visiting Zechariah while he was performing priestly duties in the Holy of Holies. Gabriel said that Zechariah and Elizabeth were going to have a child, they were to call him John, and he would go before the Lord with a spirit of power. Zechariah didn't believe it because of their ages, and because of his doubt he was struck silent until after the baby was born. Elizabeth went into seclusion for five months . . . pregnant late in life with a silent husband . . . I'm guessing that was a bit of a difficult time!

Young Mary hurried to Elizabeth's home—she needed the comfort and wisdom of this older female relative during this time. But maybe Elizabeth needed Mary too. Luke 1:41–42 says, "When Elizabeth heard Mary's greeting, the baby leaped in her womb, and Elizabeth was filled with the Holy Spirit. In a loud voice she exclaimed: 'Blessed are you among women, and blessed is the child you will bear!'" Elizabeth knew that this yet unborn child in Mary's womb was her Lord! And Mary, though she likely didn't "feel" very pregnant yet, had spent every day with this secret since the angelic message that she was to be with child by the Holy Spirit . . . young, uncertain, and likely worrying how it all could be true.

She saw Elizabeth and didn't have to explain her situation—Elizabeth knew! What a beautiful thing that God had done for these women. Mary needed an older, wiser person she could trust with her secret who loved her unconditionally. And for Elizabeth—maybe this was the encouragement she needed to come out of seclusion and face what was yet to come.

I truly believe that God doesn't mean for us to go through this life alone. We need one another. We need people in our lives we can confide in, share our concerns with, laugh and cry with. If you're feeling overwhelmed, if worry and anxious thoughts are keeping you up at night—seek out someone you can confide in to pray for you and help to carry your load. And if someone seeks you out for that support—encourage and bless that person with God's unfailing love.

Jesus, our Savior, help us to embrace the hope that you brought to the world, inspiring us to share your love with others and be beacons of light in a world that desperately needs it.

Reflect: Who are the people you go to for comfort in the midst of worry?

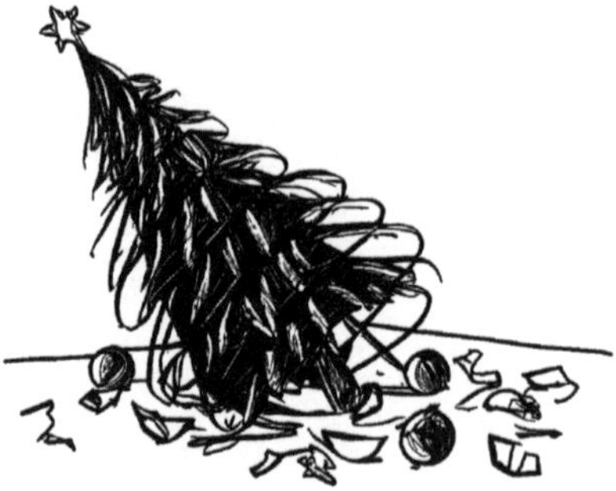

December 5

"And Mary said: 'My soul glorifies the Lord and my spirit rejoices in God my Savior, for he has been mindful of the humble state of his servant.'" —Luke 1:46–48

If you know me, I'm pretty sure you've noticed that I'm a little bit short on one end. I came to my full height in about seventh grade—just over five feet tall. Over the years, I've learned to compensate, figuring out what to do when being taller would be great. I've been known to climb a shelf at the grocery store to get something that most adults could easily reach. I always have a stool nearby in my kitchen for top-shelf items. Sometimes, I've had to climb on the counter—but that's easier said than done at this point in my life.

Literally or figuratively, we all feel small sometimes . . . insignificant, unimportant, less than, unnoticed, as if we've faded into the background of life. It occurs in relationships, careers and the workplace, school, society in general. And it can feel a little hopeless.

The Christmas story, at closer look, is a beautiful message of hope for the small and seemingly insignificant. It begins in the small village of Nazareth. In this little town lived a young girl, Mary, and her carpenter fiancé, Joseph. God saw fit that this young couple—who likely had little formal education and certainly no great financial means—would bear and raise his Son. No one would ever be more connected to the Divine. Divinity would literally reside in Mary's body. She would give birth to him, nurse him, rock him, change him, sing to him, and teach him. We are not sure how long Joseph lived—we can assume that he taught Jesus his trade and cared for him as long as he was able. We do know that in the years to come, Mary would be by Jesus' side, follow him, fear for him, and cry for him. And thirty-three years after his birth, her heart would break at the foot of the cross for him. Then with unimaginable joy, she would come to the full realization that he was just who God had promised—Jesus, who would save his people from their sins. She would see with her own eyes that he had conquered death in victory over the grave.

Jesus, God Incarnate, Immanuel, came to this earth to bring hope to the "less than," mercy to the sinner, and good news for all people. There is grace for every one of us, no matter how small, insignificant, or unimportant we might feel at any time. The great God of the universe knows your name and is offering his grace and hope to you in the person of his Son, Jesus. May we, as Mary did, glorify the Lord, for he has been mindful of our humble state and offers us unfailing love and amazing grace.

Lord Jesus, as we reflect on your humble entry into this world, let the hope that Christmas brings ignite a renewed sense of purpose and direction in our lives.

Reflect: When you think of hope at Christmas, what are the greatest longings of your heart?

December 6

"Wait for the LORD; be strong and take heart and wait for the LORD." —Psalm 27:14

Most families seem to have their own traditions during this season. Our family has always been big on watching certain movies leading up to Christmas. For us, some of the "must watch" films are *National Lampoon's Christmas Vacation, A Christmas Carol, A Charlie Brown Christmas, It's a Wonderful Life,* and of course—*White Christmas.*

The movie tells the story of the retired Army general, Thomas Waverly. He kind of loses his identity after retirement. He is running an inn in Vermont, and it's vital that there is snow for the holidays or no one will come and one of his busiest seasons will be a bust. A couple of men who served under the general have been traveling and doing musical numbers across the country. So they—and two sisters who are also entertainers—decide to take their show to the inn. They then invite soldiers and their families to come, surprising this beloved general. But the days leading up to the show on Christmas Eve are particularly warm, and there is zero snow on the ground. To the general and those working at the inn, it's looking rather bleak. Disappointment is high and expectations are low.

And how often do we experience those feelings during the month of December? We picture the perfect family Christmas and it turns out to be quite different from the Norman Rockwell depictions of the season. There are unmet expectations, someone gets sick, some of the family can't come, gifts don't satisfy. There are so many things that are out of our control.

The general needs something totally out of his control: he desperately needs it to snow. What he doesn't yet know is that in the waiting for a weather miracle, there will be one of another sort.

The people of God had been waiting for centuries for the promised Messiah, and it was totally out of their control. And when God sent an angel to Mary, and then to Joseph, to say that the promise was going to be fulfilled in them, it likely felt like they were not in control of that situation either.

Waiting. Waverly was waiting, hoping for snow. The people were looking for the long-awaited Messiah. Mary and Joseph waited for nine months to see how this was going to work out. The Psalmist declares: "Be strong and take heart and wait for the LORD."

The general is completely surprised by a full inn that night. There was a spectacular show of support from the soldiers and families who have come to honor him. And right on cue, the show begins to fall as the doors are opened wide to a winter wonderland.

I'm not sure what Mary and Joseph's expectations were, but we can assume they were met with many unexpected surprises. Having to travel to another town when Mary was due to have her child, finding no available room, birthing the Son of God among the animals and laying him in a feeding trough—these would have likely been furthest from their minds.

Whatever your expectations and longings are at this time, maybe there should be a reordering of your focus. We would love (as the song says) for all our days to be merry and bright, and all of our Christmases to be white. But as we anticipate the family celebrations, special events, and gatherings, may our deepest longing be for the kingdom of God to be realized in our lives through the person of Jesus Christ. Jesus will show up and never disappoint.

Gracious God, may the hope of Christmas guide us through the darkness of uncertainty, leading us closer to you and reminding us that your promises are true and steadfast.

Reflect: When is a time that you had to wait for God to fulfill his promises? Did he come through?

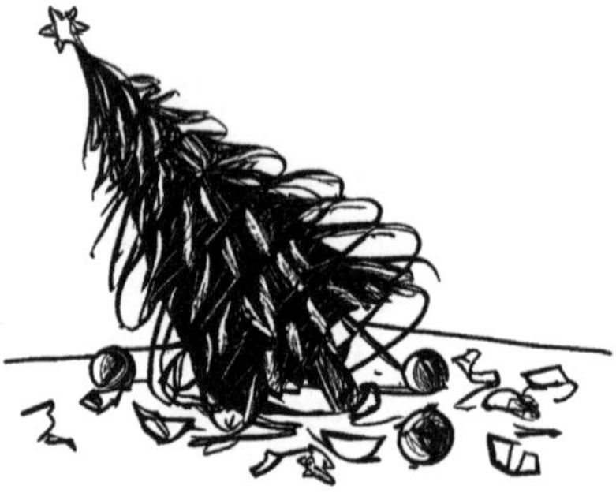

December 7

"And he will be called Wonderful Counselor, Mighty God, Everlasting Father, Prince of Peace." —Isaiah 9:6

Music has always been very important in the life of my husband, Dean, and me. As we raised our boys, we instilled a love for music in them as well. Christmas music always began to be played in our house long before December. We had lots of favorites during this season, we attended concerts of some favorite artists, and we all—at different times and places—sang some of these favorite songs during the Christmas season in church services.

Chris Rice wrote a song a number of years ago that has become one of my favorite songs of the Christmas season—but really, it is applicable to every day of the year. Musical artists such as Amy Grant and Michael W. Smith have recorded their own renditions of the song, and our youngest son, Jake, sang it for several of my Christmas Eve services when I was a pastor.

This song basically sums up the desperate need for Jesus to come into our broken world, our messed-up lives, and our violent tendencies, and bring the peace that only he can provide. Take a moment today to search for the song "Welcome to Our World." Listen to one of the recordings of it, or simply search for the lyrics online. May this song be our prayer—for ourselves, our families, our churches, our communities, our nation, and the world.

Heavenly Father, may the hope we find in the birth of Christ empower us to face the challenges ahead with unwavering trust, knowing that you are with us always.

Reflect: In the excitement of "getting things" at Christmas, what are you most looking forward to receiving from the Christ child?

December 8

"'Do not be afraid. I bring you good news that will cause great joy for all the people.' . . . Suddenly a great company of the heavenly host appeared with the angel, praising God and saying, 'Glory to God in the highest heaven, and on earth peace to those on whom his favor rests.'" —Luke 2:10, 13–14

This proclamation came from an angel to the shepherds on the hillside the night that Jesus was born. If you read over the accounts of the main characters in the Christmas story in Matthew and Luke, you will find that there was a proclamation of "Do not be afraid" a number of times—to Zechariah, Mary, Joseph, and then to the shepherds as well. Each of them had unsettling events unraveling in their lives, and they were assured that they did not need to be afraid. God was orchestrating all these things to come together in a beautiful way to usher in the miracle of his own Son's entrance into the world. And this child would grow up to be the one who would embody unfailing love, perfect peace, and a deep joy that goes far beyond circumstances.

For a number of years as a pastor in my most recent appointment, I helped to lead Advent Bible school for the children of our church and community. We met weekly leading up to the Sunday before Christmas and generally would start the evening with asking the kids, "How many days until Christmas?" Generally most of them, even many of the youngest, knew exactly how many days, and their excitement grew every week. The adults in the room knew as well—but they were usually a little more anxious or unnerved by how near it was.

And that's typical of us, of course. Wouldn't it be nice to go back in time and just enjoy the season without all the lists, planning, shopping, decorating, and preparing? And then if you add into the mix of this season difficulties at work, relationships, illness, financial stress, or loss, it can be incredibly overwhelming and anything but joyful or peace-filled.

Pause with me for a moment. . . . It's almost Christmas, but not quite yet. Yes, there is much to do. But right now, in this moment, imagine Jesus tapping you on your shoulder, trying to get your attention to focus on him. He is whispering to you—*I know your list is long: things to do, places to go, situations that need attention, hurdles to get over. I see your anxiousness and I know your fears, frustrations, and exhaustion.*

Do not be anxious or afraid, he says. *I came to the world over two thousand years ago to bring peace. This peace is not as the world might give; it's not temporary or partial. This is a deep peace that heals the broken-hearted, binds up your wounds, mends things torn and broken. It's an everlasting peace that covers your sin with forgiveness and transforms your life from feeling empty and not quite whole to one restored and redeemed—made whole by my coming into the world to bring divine love to your soul.*

May we all take time to rest in this truth during this Advent season.

"And the peace of God, which transcends all understanding, will guard your hearts and minds in Christ Jesus" (Philippians 4:7).

Heavenly Father, as we celebrate the birth of the Prince of Peace, may his presence fill our hearts and bring tranquility to our souls, spreading peace throughout the world.

Reflect: What are the areas of your life in which you have the deepest need to feel the peace of Christ?

December 9

"He will stand and shepherd his flock in the strength of the LORD, in the majesty of the name of the LORD his God. And they will live securely, for then his greatness will reach to the ends of the earth. And he will be our peace." —Micah 5:4–5a

We think of peace (or the lack thereof) in a number of ways as it affects our lives on many levels. Watch five or ten minutes of local or national news and you are not likely to hear about peace. There is war and conflict within and between nations, violence in faraway lands and just around the corner. There is injustice, prejudice, and intolerance in this world . . . and bringing it closer to home, there is conflict in relationships, abuse, betrayal . . . all in all, a great deal of heartache. And even within our own hearts and minds there are feelings of unsettledness, depression, and anxiousness that affect our relationships and our own state of mind and well-being.

Before Jesus was born, it was prophesied that the Messiah to come would be the bearer of divine peace. Throughout his ministry, he brought peace and healing to the hurting, the sinners, the broken, and the lost. As his earthly ministry was coming to a close, as the cross was looming near, he comforted his disciples and explained that things were going to change, but it would all be OK. "A time is coming and in fact has come when you will be scattered, each to your own home. You will leave me all alone. Yet I am not alone, for my Father is with me. I have told you these things so that in me you may have peace. In this world you will have trouble. But take heart! I have overcome the world" (John 16:32–33).

Jesus needed for them to know that true peace was not simply the absence of war or conflict. The Hebrew word, *shalom,* that that we translate as "peace" has a much more complex meaning. It was and is used as a greeting word, but it is also defined as peace and health that is complete or perfect. True peace is found in the person of Jesus himself, the Son of God, our Redeemer, our Restorer and our Savior, full of grace and peace.

When Jesus is invited into our hearts, we can have deep peace in the midst of whatever might be going on in our lives, our communities, our nation, and our world because Jesus *himself* is our peace for today, tomorrow, and all eternity. Make room in your heart for the Prince of Peace to take up residence and bring you the peace that passes understanding.

Lord Jesus, in this season of goodwill, may the peace that surpasses all understanding guard our minds and hearts, enabling us to reconcile with one another and embrace unity.

Reflect: How have you experienced the peace of Christ in difficult situations?

December 10

"Blessed are the peacemakers, for they will be called children of God." —Matthew 5:9

In *How NOT to Ruin Christmas*, Dan Metzger suggests to us that the opposite of peace is not violence—it's insistence. And oh, how true that is—and not only during the Christmas season, but all year long. Insistence on getting our own way, letting people know how right we are, and putting our own needs and wants ahead of everyone else does nothing for any sort of peaceful relationships. The apostle Paul instructed the church in Philippi, "Have the same mindset as Christ Jesus: Who, being in very nature God, did not consider equality with God something to be used to his own advantage; rather, he made himself nothing by taking the very nature of a servant, being made in human likeness. And being found in appearance as a man, he humbled himself..." (Philippians 2:5–8).

Acting in such a manner takes intentional effort. Humility, treating others with grace and and kindness, and putting others first, does not tend to come naturally to us. Swallowing our pride takes practice. But it is attainable with close communion with Jesus, and a determination to be the kind of Christian witness he is calling us to be. We need to take the time to pray over our days, asking God to help us speak and act with grace, mercy, and love.

Years ago, a prayer was written that is timeless in its message. Take a few minutes to ponder over these words. Then be intentional as you go about this Christmas season and beyond to offer yourself to be a peacemaking child of God.

> Lord, make me an instrument of your peace:
> where there is hatred, let me sow love;
> where there is injury, pardon;
> where there is doubt, faith;
> where there is despair, hope;
> where there is darkness, light;
> where there is sadness, joy.
> O divine Master, grant that I may not so much seek
> to be consoled as to console,
> to be understood as to understand,
> to be loved as to love.
> For it is in giving that we receive,
> it is in pardoning that we are pardoned,
> and it is in dying that we are born to eternal life.

Gracious God, as we gather with family and friends, let the peace of Christmas reign in our homes, fostering harmony, forgiveness, and love among all who dwell there.

Reflect: In what ways can you help to bring the peace of Christ to those who need it most?

December 11

*"Do not grieve, for the joy of the LORD is your strength." —
Nehemiah 8:10b*

Pastor and author Matthew Rawle, in his book *The Heart That Grew Three Sizes*, says this: "When the weather starts to turn colder, the music on the radio station changes, and my neighbors start to put lights on their homes, I have this almost giddy excitement. I always have in my head that THIS Christmas is going to be the best Christmas ever. I am certain that the kids will be overwhelmed with joy over the gifts they receive. My congregation will fill the pews and be so exuberant that the sanctuary will be just as full come Sunday. . . ." Then he says, "Why do I do this to myself?"[1]

I have been guilty of the same thing over the years when it comes to the realm of the Advent season in the church, gift-giving, and family gatherings. I think many of us have super-high expectations of the season, only to be disappointed when things go a different direction.

When the Advent season of 2020 came, the difficulty, frustration, disappointment, and unmet expectations rose to a whole new level. What was supposed to be the most wonderful time of the year found most churches (including where I served) doing services virtually. I was recording services in a mostly empty sanctuary with no congregational singing of Christmas carols, and no Advent Bible school or special events. But I was actually looking forward to our Christmas Eve service. In the spring of 2020, we got the idea to try something different for the warmer months during Covid shutdown. A gentleman from the church built a movable platform, my husband researched and purchased an FM transmitter, our praise band got onboard, and we had services in the church parking lot. Many stayed in their cars and listened on the radio, and on warm mornings, some sat outside their cars with their families. The gentleman who built the platform had the idea that he could make an enclosure around it (you know, kind of like the Popemobile) and we could use it for a Christmas Eve service. We could even put a little heater in it if it were especially cold. So I prepared the service, the praise band was willing to brave the cold and sing a few songs outside, and we would pass out glow-sticks to everyone for when we sang "Silent Night." As we spread the word, the congregation was getting excited to actually feel at least somewhat a part of the traditional Christmas Eve service.

On December 23, I woke up not feeling well. I went to a nearby urgent care clinic, where they tested me for Covid. Thirty minutes later I got the results on the app on my phone. It was positive. No Christmas Eve service for Dean and me, and all of our family gatherings were postponed. The glimmer of hope for a joyful Christmas celebration during a difficult time in the world was extinguished in a moment for me. Thankfully, I had the service scripted, and the leader of the praise band was willing to step in and make the service happen without me.

And you know what? Christmas still came. Just like with the Whos down in Whoville after everything for the Christmas celebration was stolen by the Grinch—Christmas came just the same. Cancelled in-person services and family gatherings, illness, and the sadness that went with it all couldn't keep Christmas from coming. For Joseph and Mary, though they were unable to find a decent place for the birth of their child, Christ still came. A humble place was provided, angels proclaimed the good news, shepherds came and worshiped. Though most of the world was unaware, Christ came just the same.

This can be a joyful, wonderful time of year even when things don't go as we initially hope. When we allow our main focus to be on the continual coming of Jesus into our lives and into our world, his light can shine in even the most sad and difficult circumstances. May the everlasting joy of the Lord be your strength this Advent season.

Heavenly Father, as we celebrate the birth of Jesus, fill our hearts with overflowing joy, knowing that in him, we find true and everlasting happiness.

Reflect: When was a time that you experienced unexpected joy?

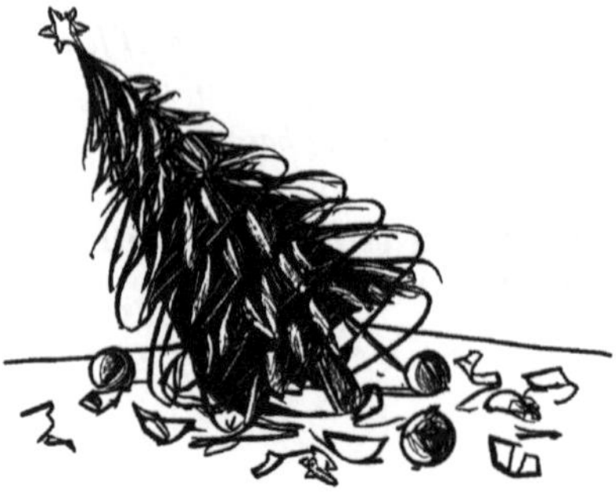

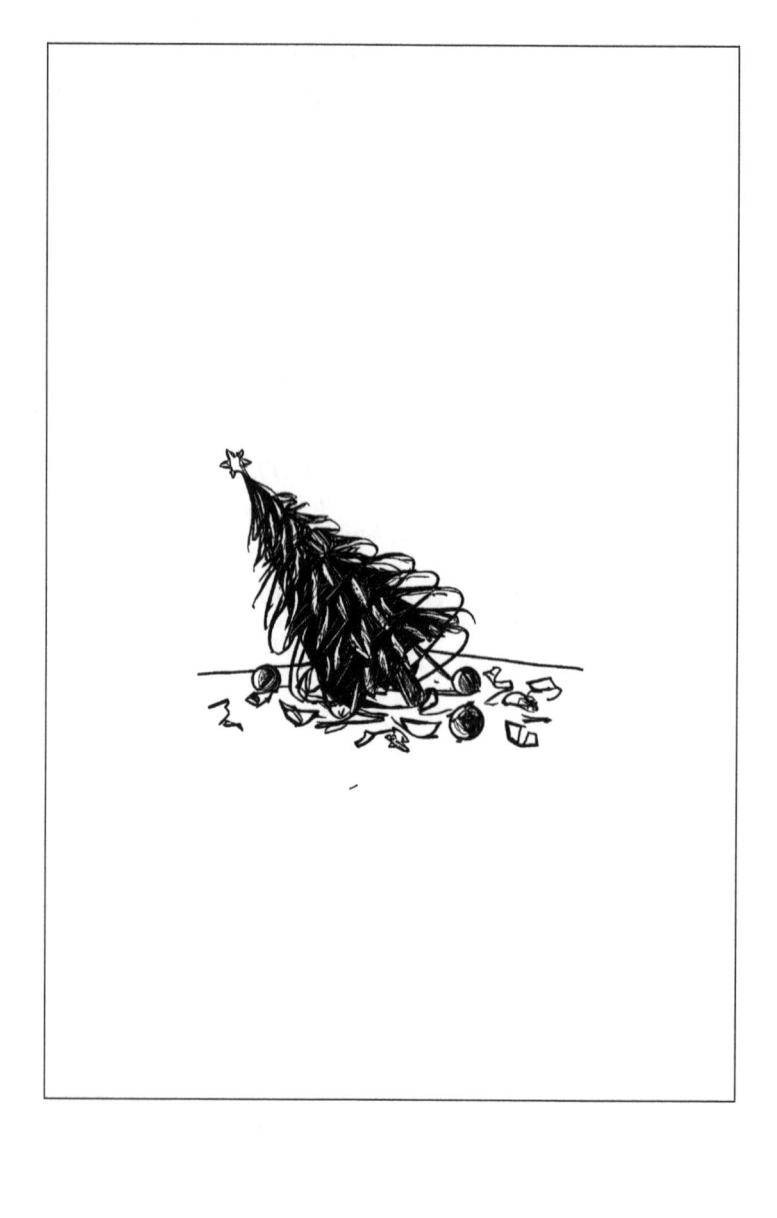

December 12

"Freely you have received; freely give."—Matthew 10:8

Long before Christmas I message my kids, their spouses, and the older grandkids and ask what they would most want for Christmas. As kids get older, they are no doubt harder and harder to buy for. Many of us spend a lot of time in stores or online trying to pick out just the right things, and we often end up frustrated at not finding the right size or things being out of stock or beyond our budget. And generally speaking, that whole process can look much more like misery than joy.

What is a gift? When it comes to the holiday season, we basically think of something purchased or made that can be put into a box and wrapped with shiny paper or placed in a holiday-decorated gift bag. Gifts are the packages around the tree and the items in the stockings. We equate packages with gifts. Maybe we need to reform our definition of *gift*.

What if this year we gave more nonpackaged gifts? A personal handwritten letter to a loved one, a phone call to someone you won't be able to see in person this year, an invitation to coffee and conversation. What if this year we chose to plan an experience with family members as a gift of joy and love that will bring enjoyment and memories for years to come? Do you remember things you gave and received last year that were wrapped in paper or placed in a pretty bag? I can recall a few things, but for the most part, the memories of last year's gift lists and shopping have faded, and it's quite likely that many of the tangible gifts that were given are no longer in use.

Jesus didn't come to us that first Christmas in the "package" that anyone anticipated the Messiah would come in. He was born in the most humble of circumstances to a young couple that had to use a feeding trough for his first crib. Wise men gave him expensive gifts—but they paled in comparison to the gift that this child would bring to the entire world.

Consider giving some gifts this year that cannot be put in a box, bag, or stocking. Share the gift of a meal for someone who is lonely and stay to eat with them. Be extra kind to the frazzled young mom in the long checkout line. Make a plan to spend a day during the next year with each of your kids or grandkids separately so they have your full attention, and do some things together that mean the most to them. Beyond opening your wallet this year, open your heart to your family, neighbors, and strangers. Give them the gift of God's unfailing love, which brings lasting joy.

Gracious God, as we gather with loved ones, may the joy of Christmas strengthen our bonds of love and deepen our appreciation for the precious relationships you have blessed us with.

Reflect: How can you help share the joy of Christ with someone today?

December 13

"Coming to his hometown, [Jesus] began teaching the people in their synagogue, and they were amazed. 'Where did this man get this wisdom and these miraculous powers?' they asked. 'Isn't this the carpenter's son?'"—Matthew 13:54–55a

The word *carpenter* used in this scripture passage is *tekton* in the Greek. It means a common laborer, someone who works with their hands, generally with wood. There are also *architektons* (where we get the word *architect*), who are master builders. In this passage, they are referring to Jesus' earthly father, Joseph, and he is simply a tekton. This is one of the very few things we know about Joseph.

There is not one recorded word of Joseph's in the Gospels. We know that he was engaged to Mary, that he received an angelic message in a dream to take Mary as his wife after she told him she was pregnant by the Holy Spirit, and that he took her to Bethlehem with him for the census, where Jesus was born. He received another angelic message to take Mary and Jesus to Egypt to escape Herod's plot to find their child and kill him, and Joseph faithfully did exactly that. When the threat was over, he received yet another message from an angel to go back home to Nazareth. The last we hear anything about Joseph is when Jesus was twelve years old and they went together to Jerusalem for the Passover.

Though we know so little about him, what we do know paints a beautiful picture of humility and faithfulness. From the very beginning of this incredible story, he simply had the faith to take Mary into his home as his wife under circumstances that must have felt very difficult to understand. And likely, as time went on and his family and friends thought about the hastened wedding and obvious state of Mary's changing body, he had to endure questioning looks and rumors of a less-than-virtuous relationship.

We talk of Mary's virtues of faithfulness and the humble act of being a faithful servant of God. I believe that when we read the ways in which Joseph acted on behalf of both her and Jesus, those same characteristics were clearly lived out in his life as well. And as they raised Jesus, I'm sure they instilled those virtues in his life, and he saw them exemplified in their words and actions.

In Matthew 20:26, 28 we read these words of Jesus: "Whoever wants to become great among you must be your servant . . . just as the Son of Man did not come to be served, but to serve, and to give his life as a ransom for many." A few days later he would wash his disciples' feet in a beautiful act of humility and service.

May we seek to have the servant heart of Jesus, Mary, and Joseph in our relationships with family, friends, neighbors, and strangers.

Lord Jesus, as we reflect on your humble arrival, teach us to find joy in simplicity and to prioritize the eternal treasures of your kingdom over the fleeting things of this world.

Reflect: Who is someone who has modeled humility for you?

December 14

"She will give birth to a son, and you are to give him the name Jesus, because he will save his people from their sins."
—Matthew 1:21

It's hard to imagine all that might have been going through Joseph's mind when he woke up from the dream after receiving this message from an angel of the Lord. The name "Jesus" in the Greek New Testament has its origin in the Old Testament, in the Hebrew name "Joshua." The name meant "Yahweh is salvation," or as we think of it in the name Jesus, "the Lord saves." Joshua of the Old Testament led the people of Israel out of the time of wandering in the wilderness into the Promised Land. In the Gospels a promise is given to Joseph and Mary that their child is to be named Jesus and that the salvation he will bring will be something everlasting. This is far greater than what was provided to the people of Israel when they were led by Joshua. Their child will be ushering in the redemption of God, which will be for all eternity.

A couple of days back, I wrote about the fact that not all gifts come in packages wrapped with a bow, shiny gift bags, or stockings. And certainly this holds true as we think of the gift of Jesus, who came to be our Savior. He came to bring us good news of great joy, to save us from our sins, and to demonstrate how to live like children of God. Then he left this world with the promise that one day we will live with him for all eternity.

There are many names that catch our attention, that make us stop and think. Some bring thoughts of awe, grace, honor, elegance, popularity, maybe even fear or disgust. Notable names: Hitler, Napoleon, Lincoln, John F. Kennedy . . . Princess Diana, Taylor Swift, Elvis, Archie Griffin, Hank Aaron . . . Caesar, Moses, Peter, Judas, Mary . . .

But there is only one name that will cause *every* knee to bow in heaven and earth and cause *every* person to confess that Jesus Christ is Lord.

His name shall be called Jesus. The Salvation of God. He saves us from sin, from our weak selves, from hopelessness and brokenness. In Jesus we experience redemption from our past, purpose for our present life, and enduring hope for the future. Jesus isn't just "the reason for the season"—the amazing gift he brought for us is the reason for every day of our lives, and the life to come.

May the powerful, comforting, peace-filled, loving, merciful name of Jesus be praised in our living, speaking, and celebrating this Advent season, and may it continue as long as we have life and breath.

Jesus, in a season when we can be so distracted, may we remember that you are the King of Kings and the Lord of Lords, and that you supply our every need.

Reflect: In what ways has knowing Jesus given you new purpose and meaning for your life?

December 15

"'The virgin will conceive and give birth to a son, and they will call him Immanuel' (which means 'God with us')."
—*Matthew 1:23*

We generally make a connection between the name Immanuel and Jesus. But the first time this name is recorded in scripture is in the book of Isaiah, and it was written over seven hundred years before Jesus' birth. At that time, Israel was a divided nation consisting of a northern kingdom and a southern kingdom. They shared history, culture, language, and religion. Sometimes they worked together, other times they were at war with each other.

This prophecy of Immanuel is found in Isaiah chapter 7. At that time the northern kingdom had an alliance with another kingdom, Aram, what is currently western Syria. Together they planned to fight against the people of the empire of Assyria, who were oppressing them with heavy taxes. But in order to be successful, they were going to need the help of Judah, the southern kingdom. However, the king of Judah, King Ahaz, refused to join in.

So the kings of Aram and the northern kingdom of Israel prepared to attack Judah—hoping to put a new leader into power who would be allies with them. The Lord tells Isaiah to go before King Ahaz and assure him they will not be defeated. Isaiah 7:14 reads, "Therefore the Lord himself will give you a sign: The virgin will conceive and give birth to a son, and will call him Immanuel." This actually referred to a young woman of Ahaz's time, and about a year later, a child was born to her.

In the next decade, the northern kingdom of Israel and the kingdom of Aram were overtaken by the Assyrians. The child, Immanuel, was the living promise that God indeed was with Ahaz and the people of Judah.

Matthew is the only one who quoted this verse from Isaiah and saw it as a powerful and important picture of Jesus, the Messiah, our Savior, Immanuel—God is with us. And though all the Gospels tell stories of Jesus' life and ministry, Matthew alone makes this strong statement in the first chapter of his Gospel. He makes clear from the beginning of his writings about Jesus that Jesus is the very presence of the almighty creator God in human form living among humankind. And we can be assured that, in living this way, he would have life experiences that are much like our own. He would know betrayal, hurt, anger, hunger, loneliness, fear. . . . He understands us.

We can know deep peace and, yes, true joy—assured that the redeemer of our souls understands and has conquered sin, death, hopelessness, and fear for us. Matthew ends his Gospel with Jesus' words, "Therefore go and make disciples of all nations, baptizing them in the name of the Father and of the Son and of the Holy Spirit, and teaching them to obey everything I have commanded you. And surely I am with you always, to the very end of the age" (Matthew 28:19–20).

He is still Immanuel. God with us, God in us, God for us. Thanks be to God.

Jesus, we thank you for coming to be with us, in the midst of the trials and tribulations of our lives, showing us your never-failing love.

Reflect: What are the ways in which you most assuredly know that God is present with you?

December 16

"And Mary said: 'My soul glorifies the Lord and my spirit rejoices in God my Savior.'" —Luke 1:46–47

Mary says these words after she greets Elizabeth, grateful for their bond as close relatives and the knowledge that they, though a number of years apart, are both carrying miracle children in their wombs. There are going to be difficult days ahead, but Mary in that moment pauses to proclaim the joy that God has blessed her spirit with.

I was the youngest of four siblings and was blessed with wonderful parents. When I got married, we moved only about ten miles away from them. It was such a blessing for our kids to have both sets of grandparents close by.

My dad died unexpectedly in 1996 when our youngest son was only four years old. My siblings all lived much further away or were unable to provide extra care for my mom at that time. I was so thankful that we lived nearby and could help her to navigate the grief and sudden changes in her life. The following year we assisted in helping her to sell her home and downsize into a condo in the same town. She adjusted well and enjoyed her time there. And though we had already had a close bond as mother and daughter, the coming years would draw us even closer.

Mom was truly one of the kindest, most faithful, most grace-filled people I have ever met. She was incredibly disciplined in Bible reading and study and had a deep prayer life. She kept journals of people and situations she was praying for. I knew that if I shared something of concern with her I could absolutely count on her prayers. She would go back into her journals and fill in notes if and when she heard how the concerns she'd written down were resolved.

Several years after Dad's passing, Mom began to seem a little confused at times and increasingly forgetful. I went with her to her family physician. He felt pretty certain she was in the early stages of Alzheimer's and put her on a medication that would hopefully slow the progression of the disease. And thankfully it did. She was able to remain in the condo, and our family did more to assist her with things that she needed additional help with. Then, in 2008, the disease had progressed to the point that it was necessary for her to no longer drive, and it was clear she needed more care than we could provide at the time. We found an assisted living facility just a few miles from our home and we moved her there. A few years later, she needed full nursing home care, and she moved within the same facility to where they could provide that for her. Her mind was failing her, but she never lost her grace-filled spirit or her joy. Eventually she could no longer read, but she faithfully prayed and went to chapel services whenever they were available. What was incredible was that she could still play the piano and read music quite well. When she moved into assisted living, we got her a full-sized keyboard instead of trying to move her piano. Every day she would play, and when she was moved to nursing home care, they put it in a common room nearby and someone would push her in the wheelchair so she could play regularly. And everyone loved the music from sweet little "Dixie" (her longtime nickname). Everyone loved her.

She taught me more life lessons than anyone else I've known. She taught me about faith, discipline, gratefulness, and kindness. And she taught me about joy. Even when words were hard to come by and her memory faded, she was joyful. Every day, up until her last breath, her spirit rejoiced in God her Savior. Thank you, Mom, for that incredible gift that will stay with me for the rest of my days.

Heavenly Father, in the midst of our sorrows and trials, grant us the gift of your abiding joy, reminding us that even in the darkest times, your light shines brightest.

Reflect: How has God comforted you in times of sorrow?

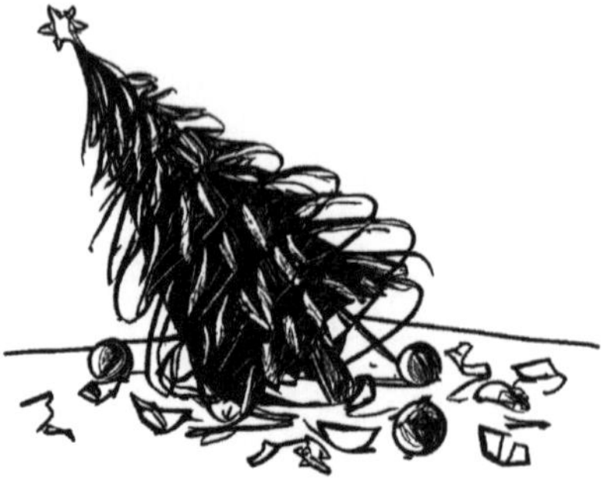

December 17

"But Mary treasured up all these things and pondered them in her heart." —Luke 2:19

In the summer of 2016, not only was my mom's mind continuing to fail, but her arthritis-ridden body was more rapidly failing as well. She could no longer stand and needed to be lifted from bed to her wheelchair and back again. We did all we could to make the most of every visit. She loved going outside, and I was so thankful for the beautiful weather that summer so I could take her out for lots of walks, pushing her wheelchair and enjoying the sunshine and gardens on the property.

She turned ninety that July, and we celebrated with her favorite treats of chocolate cake and ice cream. I certainly inherited my love of all things chocolate from her. But she always had far more willpower than I ever had, being able to eat just a small piece of cake or a little piece of a Hershey bar. She was always smiling and loved every moment that family members came to visit. Mom always professed her love for us and thanked us for just being there with her whenever we could. The staff at the facility adored her, as she was always kind and grateful for everything they did for her.

As the calendar turned to September, it became evident that she would likely not be in our lives much longer. She was down to below ninety pounds and was having great difficulty swallowing. The final week of her life, she was bedridden and ate only a couple of bites of food a day, and that was only with assistance from myself or nursing staff.

Early on the morning of September 23 we received a call that Mom had had a very rough night and that we should come as quickly as we could. Dean and I went immediately to be with her. She was awake and attempted to communicate, but physically her body was exhausted and weak. Mom was in a room with another lady, and I requested that she be moved to a different room so we could have privacy during this critical time. They moved her right away, and Dean left for a short appointment and would be quickly returning. I texted our kids and asked them to pray that she wouldn't suffer long in this state. Our youngest son was the only one who lived close by at that time, and he said he would be there soon.

As I sat in the room holding Mom's hand and praying, the sun rose, and its light glowed in the window. Her breathing was slowing, so I just laid my hand on her chest and told her how much I loved her and that it was OK, she could fly to Jesus. Within minutes she peacefully slipped from this earth into the arms of God. Dean and our son didn't make it in time. But maybe that was how it was meant to be. I will never forget being with her as her breathing slowed and stopped and all her struggle ended.

The weeks and months ahead were rough for me. The day of Mom's funeral, a dear lady from my church died, and a few days later I officiated at her funeral. I plodded my way through the busy fall and Advent season of the church, all while navigating the deep grief of losing my dear mom. In mid-December I spoke with our church leadership and told them I desperately needed to take some time off after Christmas for some rest and self-care, to which they readily agreed.

My family knew how difficult a time it had been for me, and of course they were grieving as well. Often it's hard to remember from year to year gifts given and received, but I will never forget what my wonderful sons and their families gave me that year. I had to open it first before anyone else opened any gifts. I was moved to tears as I opened up a box with a small Christmas tree that was decorated with special ornaments that reminded them of Mom. There were birds, squirrels, Snoopy figures, a piano, and a Cleveland Indians ornament. Since then I've picked up a few more to add that remind me especially of her. And I leave it up all year round.

That Christmas, we shared tears, laughter, and lots of blessed memories of Mom and held her close to our hearts. If you are grieving a loss this Advent season—whether recent or long past—make the time to be with those who can lift your spirits and share their memories. If you know of someone else in that situation this year, do all you can to support them and walk the journey with them.

Lord Jesus, as we navigate through seasons of loss and grief, fill our hearts with the joy of your presence, comforting us with the assurance that you are the source of our strength and the healer of our wounds.

Reflect: How do the cherished memories of loved ones help us to experience Christ at Christmas?

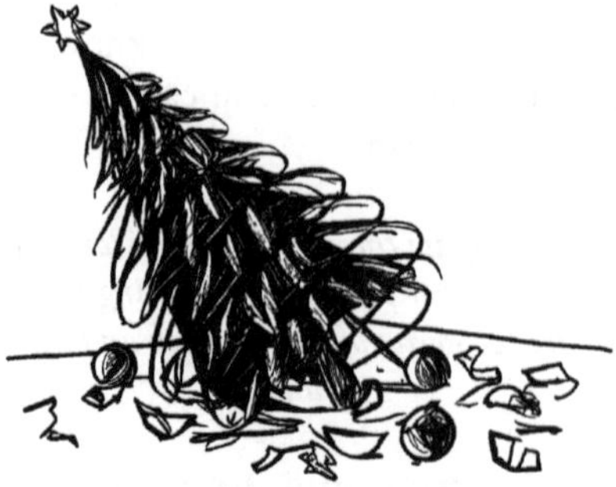

December 18

"And there were shepherds living out in the fields nearby, keeping watch over their flocks at night."—Luke 2:8

In *The Nativity Story*,[2] a movie that dramatizes the Christmas story, there is a scene close to the time of the birth of Jesus as Mary and Joseph are approaching Bethlehem. There is an older shepherd sitting by the side of the road with a small lamb, and he encourages them to stop there with him so Mary can rest a little bit. In their conversation, the shepherd says that his father once told him that everyone has been given a gift. He tells Mary that her gift is the child she is carrying inside her. Mary then asks what his gift is, to which he replies—only the hope of finding it someday. Shortly after that they move on so they can get to Bethlehem before nightfall.

After Jesus is born in the movie comes a scene of the angel appearing to the shepherds on the hillside and many of them beginning their walk to the scene of the birth. The shepherd Mary and Joseph encountered is the first to enter the cave and kneel before Jesus. Mary then holds Jesus toward him, allowing him to reach out and touch the cloths the baby is wrapped in, and she tells him, "We have all been given a gift."

Though of course this is part of the dramatized story, I love that it is included to enhance the beautiful story of the shepherds. Shepherds during that time were certainly not regarded highly. Though they were very important to their culture for providing wool, meat, and animals for sacrifices, they were looked at as uneducated and simple. They lived among their animals, so they were not likely to smell very good or be clean and tidy.

Why do you think that God chose lowly shepherds living out in the fields around Bethlehem to be the first to witness the miracle birth of his one and only Son? The proclamation of the angel helps to answer this question. The angel said, "Do not be afraid. I bring you good news that will cause great joy for all the people. Today in the town of David a Savior has been born to you; he is the Messiah, the Lord" (Luke 2:10–11).

Jesus came for everyone, from the lowest rung of society to royalty. Everyone has been offered this precious gift. And God chose these basically unseen shepherds to be seen by the God of the universe and the Child who would one day offer them the gift of salvation by dying on the cross for them. Their humble lives were rewarded—an important lesson for all of us. "Humble yourselves before the Lord, and he will lift you up" (James 4:10).

Gracious God, may the love exemplified in the manger stir our hearts to love you more deeply, to love ourselves with humility, and to love our neighbors as ourselves, embracing the commandment you have given us.

Reflect: Have there been times when God has "lifted you up" into situations that you felt were more than you deserved?

December 19

"So they hurried off and found Mary and Joseph, and the baby, who was lying in the manger. When they had seen him, they spread the word concerning what had been told them about this child, and all who heard it were amazed at what the shepherds said to them. But Mary treasured up all these things and pondered them in her heart. The shepherds returned, glorifying and praising God for all the things that they had heard and seen, which were just as they had been told." —Luke 2:16–20

We can't be exactly sure how far the shepherds had to travel to find Jesus—but we do have this record that they quickly headed into the town of Bethlehem, trusting that what the angel had proclaimed to them was true. It could be that some stayed behind to tend to the flocks, but we don't have that information in the scripture text either. Arriving at the place of Jesus' birth, they found it to be just as the angels had told them.

We don't dwell as much on what followed the moment they saw Jesus for themselves, but it is certainly important to make note of. These shepherds spread the word about the miracle of what they had just witnessed. From what we know of how shepherds at that time were viewed, people might not have listened, believed what they were saying, or paid much attention to them. But scripture says that all who heard it were amazed. That could possibly be because there were a number of them and they all had the exact same story, which made it more believable. However, I wonder if there was another, or an additional, explanation.

This moment in their lives seems to have transformed them. They could not contain the joy they felt and didn't stop to think how the people might react to them. God had given them an unimaginable gift, and they simply could not keep it to themselves. The shepherds felt compelled to share the good news with whoever they encountered. Wonder and praise overflowed from their transformed hearts and lives. And all the people who experienced their witness were amazed.

During this month, and sometimes for weeks and months prior to December, many people search for the perfect gifts for the special people in their lives. And though there is nothing wrong with that, maybe we need to think about those who would benefit from us sharing the greatest gift of all with them. Is the joy of knowing the Christ of Christmas so prevalent in our lives that it overflows to others? Are our hearts so full of the love and grace of Jesus that we simply can't keep it to ourselves?

As Christmas Day draws near, may we all seek out people to share the good news of great joy with. As the shepherds did, may we praise and glorify God and intentionally share the precious gift of Jesus.

Heavenly Father, may the joyous tidings of the angels resound in our souls, reminding us that through Christ, we are recipients of your abundant grace and unending joy.

Reflect: Can you remember a time you were lost in amazement at the things God was doing in your life?

December 20

"She gave birth to her firstborn, a son. She wrapped him in cloths and placed him in a manger, because there was no guest room available for them." —Luke 2:7

Matthew and Luke both mention that Jesus was born in Bethlehem, but only Luke specifically mentions that he was placed in a manger. This certainly pointed to Jesus' very humble beginning to his earthly life. Not only were Mary and Joseph unable to find a decent place to stay on the night he was born, but they were obviously among animals of some sort for there to have been a manger—a feeding trough for animals in the only place they could find. As a parent, it is truly hard for me to comprehend being in such a situation when it is time for a child to be born. Nevertheless, the God of the universe was making it clear that his Son came into the world to identify with the meek, the poor, and the humble.

Is there perhaps more significance to these circumstances than initially meets the eye? We cannot know exactly why Luke might have mentioned the manger three times when telling Jesus' birth story, but we can definitely make connections to some significant events in his ministry.

We do know that Bethlehem, the place of Jesus' birth, means "House of Bread" and that Jesus was placed in a manger, which would have held food for animals. We also know of stories from the Gospels when Jesus multiplied small loaves of bread to feed thousands of people. And sometime shortly after one of those events, we have these recorded words of Jesus: "I am the bread of life. Whoever comes to me will never go hungry, and whoever believes in me will never be thirsty. . . . I am the living bread that came down from heaven. Whoever eats this bread will live forever. This bread is my flesh, which I will give for the life of the world" (John 6:35, 51). And then on the night he was arrested, Jesus shared a meal with his disciples, and breaking the bread, he declared, "This is my body given for you; do this in remembrance of me" (Luke 22:19).

It would seem that Luke's specific mention of the manger points not only to Jesus' humble beginnings but also to the fact that Jesus himself came to offer to all of us the divine bread that would satisfy the deepest needs of our hearts. Our hunger for fulfillment in this life can only be satisfied in the person of Jesus. There may be lots of gifts under your tree this year, but none will bring full, lasting, and eternal joy.

May you find deep peace, and may your soul be full and satisfied with the Christ of Christmas, the Bread of Life.

Heavenly Father, as we celebrate Christmas, we thank you for sending Jesus, the Bread of Life, whose birth sustains our souls and nourishes us with eternal hope.

Reflect: How have you experienced Jesus satisfying your soul in ways that nothing else can?

December 21

"In him was life, and that life was the light of all mankind. The light shines in the darkness, but the darkness has not overcome it." —John 1:4–5

Though we celebrate the Advent season during the month of December, there is not an actual record of exactly what time of year Jesus was born. And though many early Christian leaders made an effort to date the birth of Jesus with thoughtful consideration, we should remember that Jesus was born in a period when time was often referred to in terms of the reign of a certain king or governmental leader, and when nature, certain festivals, and symbolism played a role in dating significant events.

One idea that has been given a lot of consideration is that the date of December 25 was chosen because of its proximity to the winter solstice, which generally falls on December 21 or 22. Up until this time, the hours and minutes of daylight have been decreasing since the summer solstice in June. Then, at the time of the winter solstice, the pattern shifts in the other direction. It's hard to perceive at first—but within the next few days, we will have gained several minutes of daylight. The light increases . . . darkness decreases.

To me, it seems perfect for us to be celebrating the birth of Jesus, the Light of the World, at a time when the light is pushing back the darkness. Jesus came into this world to do just that for us all.

The prophet Isaiah proclaimed, "The people walking in darkness have seen a great light; on those living in the land of deep darkness, a light has dawned" (Isaiah 9:2).

The psalmist David said, "The Lord is my light and my salvation—whom shall I fear? The Lord is the stronghold of my life—of whom shall I be afraid?" (Psalm 27:1).

When Simeon held the baby Jesus in the Temple, he said, "Sovereign Lord, as you have promised, you may now dismiss your servant in peace. For my eyes have seen your salvation, which you have prepared in the sight of all nations: a light for revelation to the Gentiles, and the glory of your people Israel" (Luke 2:29–32).

Jesus declared, "I am the light of the world. Whoever follows me will never walk in darkness, but will have the light of life" (John 8:12).

Jesus came to push back the darkness in our lives, in whatever forms it might come to us: the darkness of sin, grief, sadness, loneliness, hopelessness, fear. . . . He wants us all to come to the light of his great love and mercy for us, to find rest in him, comfort in his presence, and hope for this life and the life to come.

It is my prayer for all who might read these words that in the midst of whatever you might be dealing with this day, you may know the light of Christ shining into the dark places of your life and circumstances. May you know the warmth and comfort of Jesus—Messiah, King, Savior, Immanuel . . . the Light of the World.

Lord Jesus, may the love that brought you from heaven to earth ignite a flame of compassion within us, prompting acts of kindness, forgiveness, and reconciliation.

Reflect: What does it mean to you to shine Jesus' light in the darkness?

December 22

"After Jesus was born in Bethlehem in Judea, during the time of King Herod, Magi from the east came to Jerusalem and asked, 'Where is the one who has been born king of the Jews? We saw his star when it rose and have come to worship him.'"—Matthew 2:1–2

There has been a lot of thought and debate on exactly what the heavenly body was that led the Magi on their journey. But whatever it was, God provided something quite visible in the sky that would serve as a travel guide for this group of travelers from the east looking for this special child to be born. And this star took them to the exact location of Mary, Joseph, and Jesus, and there they bowed down and worshiped, offering their finest gifts. Without divine guidance they would never have reached this destination.

I've been thinking recently about the "stars" in my life who provided divine guidance to me that ultimately led me to faith in Jesus and a continual journey of walking with him in this life. From my childhood I remember a particular pastor, the Rev. Rolland Perkins, who had a large impact on my young life. He was my confirmation teacher and helped to instill in me a love for the church. Not long after that, I was blessed with a wonderful youth pastor who became a friend of our family and did a great deal to assist me in a deeper walk with Jesus. And no doubt, most influential of all was my mom. Her daily devotion to God and her willingness and patience to answer my many questions inspired me to dig deeper into scripture. Her example of kindness, grace, and faith will be with me forever.

Take some time in these remaining days of Advent to pause to reflect on those stars in your life, the divine travel guides that God has provided for you as you are on your journey with Jesus. Be thankful to God, and thank them personally if you are able. Those people are timeless gifts in our lives. And if you are early in your Christian walk, I encourage you to reach out to God in prayer for guidance. Then open your eyes and heart and look around you—chances are there is a person or persons you can look to whose faith and love are inspiring to you.

God gave a message to Jeremiah, who gave it to the people: "Call on me and come and pray to me, and I will listen to you. You will seek me and find me when you seek me with all your heart. I will be found by you" (Jeremiah 29:12–14a).

When you read about the Christmas star or see it depicted on Christmas cards and in nativity scenes, be reminded that when you seek Jesus, you will be given divine guidance on your journey. You will find God.

Gracious God, in this season of giving, teach us to extend love beyond our immediate circles, reaching out to the marginalized, the lonely, and the broken-hearted, embodying the true spirit of Christmas.

Reflect: Who has been a guiding star for you? For whom do you provide guidance?

December 23

"On coming to the house, they saw the child with his mother Mary, and they bowed down and worshiped him. Then they opened their treasures and presented him with gifts of gold, frankincense and myrrh." —Matthew 2:11

I love the story of the Magi and all that it conjures up in my mind. And my imagination is affected as much by modern nativity scenes and Christmas pageants as by Matthew's Gospel account. It's almost certain the Magi didn't arrive the day Jesus was born, as the shepherds did. They likely arrived days, weeks, or even months later. They didn't find Jesus in the manger but found him in a home where the young family was staying after the birth and before their escape to Egypt. Also we don't know for sure if there were three Magi. There were at least two, but there could have been several more. There were three gifts mentioned, but we can't be certain exactly how many men. Still, I love the image in my mind of a brilliant star and people who traveled a great distance bowing before Jesus with awe on their faces and magnificent gifts in their hands.

Although the story of these Wise Men is embellished by songs, nativity scenes, and much speculation about their origin, we can certainly learn much from them today. They were chosen to have an intimate encounter with the Son of God, and no doubt their lives were forever changed.

I think one of the most important things we learn from their part in the nativity story is that God is reaching out to us no matter where we are, how far we may be from him, or what our background is. Most every biblical scholar will say that these men were not Jews, but much more likely were Gentiles. They didn't necessarily grow up in the Jewish faith—at least not that we know of. And I'm pretty sure they didn't go to worship services or attend Bible studies. They were likely astrologers who studied the stars. Their lives took an incredible turn when God caused them to observe this star and begin the journey to find someone they understood to be a new king. God reached down to these people, exactly where they were, and somehow made himself and his mission known to them. And he used a means that they would understand—an astronomical event signaling them to search for the child born the king of the Jews. The Jewish people believed the coming Messiah would be for them, to deliver them personally, and now this message was delivered to some astrologers living far away from them.

The message still rings true today—there is never anyone so far from God that he cannot reach them. If God could reach Gentile astrologers living far from where Jesus was born, we can be assured that he is still reaching toward people who may think they are too far gone. God never gives up on anyone and uses whatever means he can to help lead them to himself, to his Son, Jesus, and to the grace he freely offers to everyone.

The Magi followed God's leading and knelt before the King of Kings, offering worship and magnificent gifts. We would have to believe they left with their lives transformed. May our encounter with the Christ of Christmas, King of Kings, Lord of Lords, and Prince of Peace transform and guide us to seek the wisdom and the heart of God all year long.

Lord Jesus, as we reflect on the encounter the Magi had with you at Christmas, open our hearts to seek you earnestly, to offer our gifts in worship, and to be forever transformed by your divine presence.

Reflect: In what new ways have you experienced the love of Christ this Advent season?

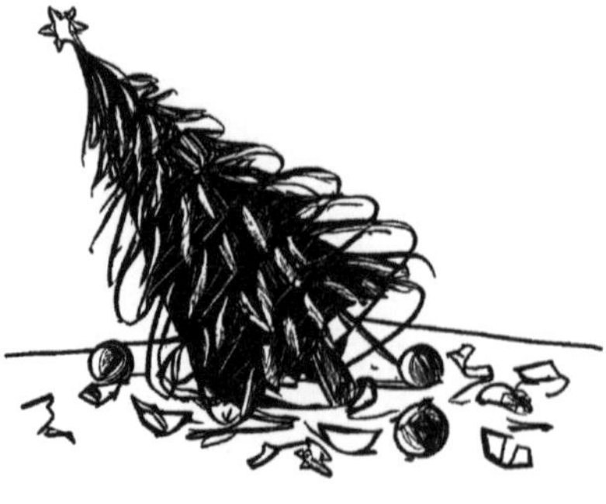

December 24

"But Mary treasured up all these things and pondered them in her heart. The shepherds returned, glorifying and praising God for all the things they had heard and seen, which were just as they had been told." —Luke 2:19–20

Many churches will sing "Silent Night" by candlelight during their Christmas Eve services. During my years of being a pastor, that was the tradition every single year at the close of the service. "Silent night, holy night; all is calm, all is bright." I loved that part of the service as I looked out across the congregation with the lights dimmed and the candles being lit from person to person. It was always a peaceful and moving experience. But I think we can be pretty sure that it was not a completely silent and calm night when Jesus was born. Mary and Joseph would have been weary from their nearly ninety-mile trip from Nazareth to Bethlehem. Mary was nine months pregnant, and there was no place for them to rest except for a stall or cave that likely had animals in it. After the birth, shepherds came to visit, possibly with some noisy little lambs in tow. It may have been anything but calm and silent.

But I wonder if there was a shift in mood and atmosphere later in the night. After the pain of the birth, after the shepherds had returned to the fields, maybe there was a time of rest for Mary and Joseph. As they reflected on the previous days and hours, maybe some much-needed peace settled over them.

Though they could not have fully understood all that was transpiring when Mary gave birth to Jesus, they knew it was a miracle and that he was, no doubt, the Son of God. Birthing the Savior would evolve into a realization that Jesus would be born in the hearts of humanity. All people are offered the gifts of deep and eternal peace, hope, joy, and unfailing love as the Christ of Christmas is born in our hearts.

Dear God, in the stillness of this holy night, may your peace and love envelop us as we gratefully celebrate the birth of our Savior, Jesus Christ.

Reflect: In what ways have you made your heart into a place for the Christ child to be born?

December 25

"Suddenly a great company of the heavenly host appeared with the angel, praising God and saying, 'Glory to God in the highest heaven, and on earth peace to those on whom his favor rests.'"—Luke 2:13–14

On December 1, I posed the question, *What are you anticipating that this month will hold for you?* Now, as you look back over this month, what stands out most to you? I'm sure there were some times of frustration when you were stuck in traffic and long checkout lines and wondering how you were going to get everything done. But I hope that as you reflect on these last several weeks, there are positive and life-giving thoughts that come to mind. Dwell on those things on this blessed Christmas Day.

Today we rejoice with the angels at the good news of great joy: that God sent to us the greatest gift of all time—his one and only Son! Jesus, Immanuel—God is with us. The God of yesterday, today, and tomorrow has been, is currently, and will always be present. When we think of the specific elements of the Advent season—hope, peace, joy, and love—we can see how the gift of the Savior coming into the world expresses all of them for all time. For us today, love is the expression of the past when "God so loved the world that he gave his one and only Son." We experience peace in the present as Jesus lives in us and walks with us on this life's journey, no matter what we might be experiencing or what our circumstances are.

Hope gives us assurance of the future, that God will continue to be with us, and of life eternal in the very presence of God through the gift of his Son. And joy is the continual river that flows in and through it all as we live mindful of the amazing grace God has blessed us with.

As the Advent season draws to a close, may the divine hope, peace, joy, and love of this time remain with you as you welcome a new year.

Joy to the world! The Lord has come, is continually coming to us every single day, and will come again in glory!

Thanks be to God for his indescribable gift!

Heavenly Father, on this Christmas Day, we gather in joy, grateful for the gift of your Son and asking for your continued blessings of hope, peace, joy, and love to fill our hearts and homes.

Reflect: On this Christmas Day, how have you discovered anew the gifts of hope, peace, joy, and love?

About the Author

Erma Metzger is a retired pastor from the West Ohio Conference of the United Methodist Church. Together with her husband Dean, she raised three sons in rural northwest Ohio. Their oldest son, Dan, is also a West Ohio Conference pastor and the author of *How NOT to Ruin Christmas*. In retirement Erma and Dean are enjoying life on the family farm, gardening, traveling, and spending time with friends and family—especially enjoying more time with their grandchildren. She counts it a privilege and blessing to have been able to collaborate with Dan on this literary project.

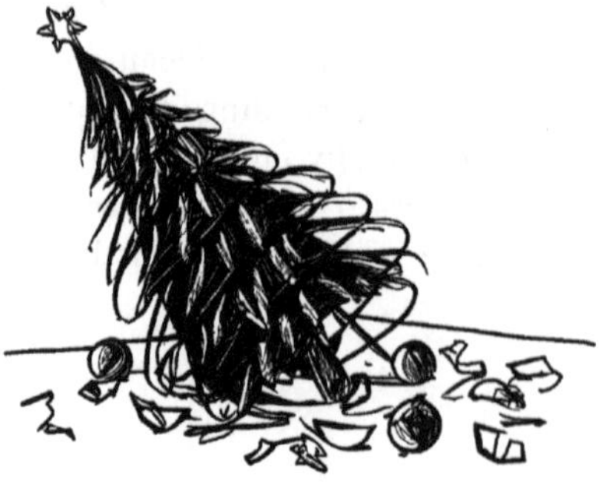

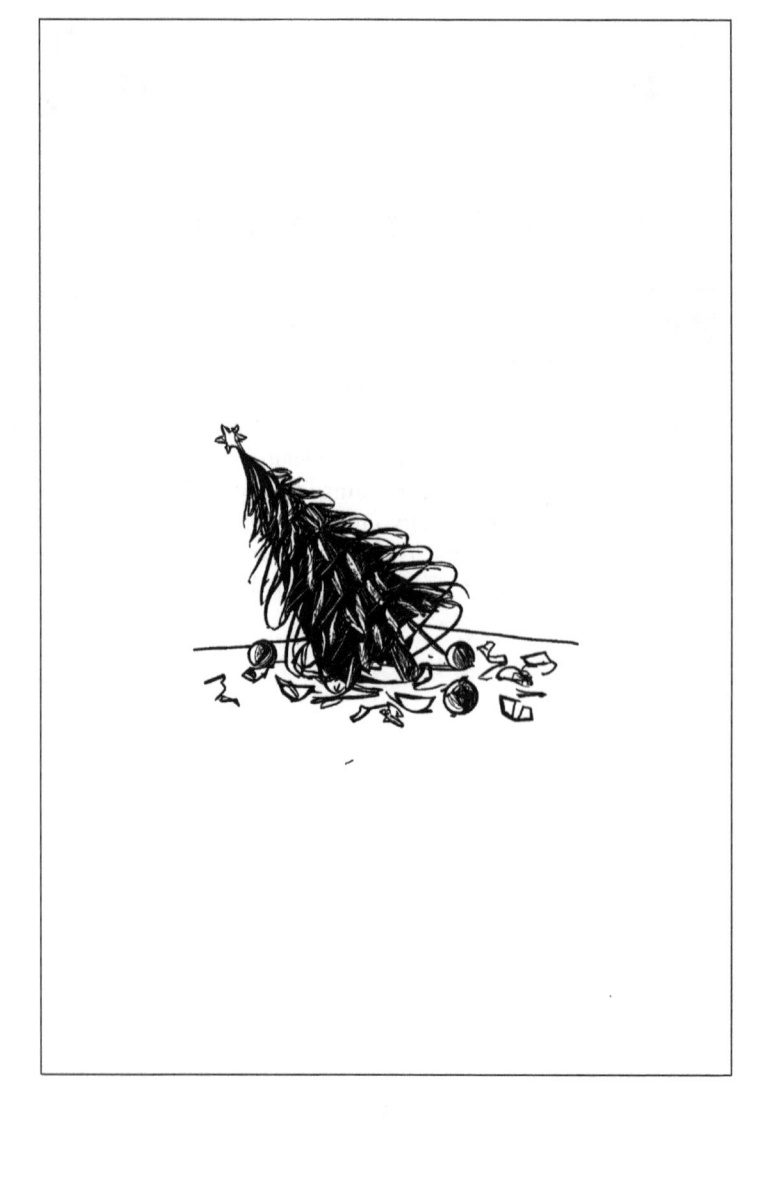

Endnotes

1. Matthew Rawle, *The Heart That Grew Three Sizes: Finding Faith in the Story of the Grinch* (Nashville: Abingdon Press, 2021), 31.

2. *The Nativity Story*, directed by Catherine Hardwicke (Temple Hill Entertainment, 2006).

SCAN HERE to learn more about Invite Press, a premier publishing imprint created to invite people to a deeper faith and living relationship with Jesus Christ.

Milton Keynes UK
Ingram Content Group UK Ltd.
UKHW020813080824
446708UK00027BA/370